The Wolves

Sarah DeLappe's play *The Wolves* premiered Off Broadway at The Playwrights Realm, following an engagement at New York Stage and Film, and development at Clubbed Thumb. It was subsequently remounted at Lincoln Center Theater. *The Wolves* received the American Playwriting Foundation's inaugural Relentless Award, and was a finalist for the 2017 Pulitzer Prize, the 2016 Susan Smith Blackburn Prize, and the Yale Drama Series Prize. She holds an MFA in Playwriting from Brooklyn College.

The Wolves

A PLAY BY

Sarah DeLappe

THE OVERLOOK PRESS
NEW YORK. NY

This edition first published in the United States in 2018 by
The Overlook Press, an imprint of ABRAMS

Copyright © 2018 by Sarah DeLappe
Design and typesetting by Bernard Schleifer

Cataloging-in-Publication Data is available from the Library of Congress.

ISBN: 978-1-4683-1571-4

Printed and bound in the United States
7 9 10 8

Abrams books are available at special discounts when purchased in quantity for premiums and promotions as well as fundraising or educational use. Special editions can also be created to specification. For details, contact specialsales@abramsbooks.com or the address below.

ABRAMS The Art of Books
195 Broadway, New York, NY 10007
abramsbooks.com

*For all the Wolves—past,
present, and future—
especially, always, Eva*

We are always the same age inside.

—GERTRUDE STEIN

Preface

I wrote this play in a sports bra. I am not an athlete in my current life and hadn't worn one since high school. I would take off my shirt, take off my bra, pull the sports bra over my chest, and sit down to write. I overshare not to advocate for method writing (although . . .) but to suggest just what sort of play this play was from the start. Physical. Concerned with the body, with women's bodies, not as eye candy or symbolic vessels but as muscular, dexterous, capable, contradictory, and fallible individuals.

Welcome to a planet of teenage girls.

The biographical fallacy hounds writers, particularly writers who happen to identify as female. Many assume that she must be writing from her own life or how else did she think of the darn thing? I did not play soccer in high school. I was a teenage girl, I knew other teenage girls, I still do. These characters are not downloaded from my yearbook. This play is not really about soccer.

So why soccer?

AstroTurf and American exceptionalism. It's essential that these girls are playing *indoor* soccer, deep in the suburbs, in a massive structure engineered to allow them to pursue this leisure activity in shirtsleeves in the dead of winter. The world's sport has been siloed to an Air Dome in a suburb. Their team is undefeated. These American teenagers exist, quite literally, in a bubble. At that particular age when the stakes of everyday life could not be higher, they are desperate to understand themselves and the world around them, but they can only see so far.

I thought of the play like a war movie. Instead of a troop of young men preparing for battle, we watch a team of young women warming up for their soccer game. There's a captain, a rebel, an innocent, a recent recruit, a common enemy. The arc follows an escalation of blood and viscera both in the content of their speech and the actual sustained injuries and traumas. Of course, their battlefield is a carpet of artificial grass.

And, yet, on their artificial grass, these girls are allowed to define themselves amongst themselves. Their bodies are their own and they are strong. We do not meet them as the property or accessory of a man—a boyfriend, a father, an institutional custodian in school or in government—we meet them with each other. We're on their turf. They're not on ours.

Sarah DeLappe
January 2018

The world premiere of *The Wolves* was produced by The Playwrights Realm (Katherine Kovner, Artistic Director; Roberta Pereira, Producing Director), at The Duke on 42nd St in New York City on September 8, 2016. The performance was directed by Lila Neugebauer, with sets by Laura Jellinek, costumes by Asta Hostetter, lights by Lap Chi Chu, sound by Stowe Nelson, and wigs by Anne Ford-Coates. The Production Stage Manager was Lori Lundquist. The cast was:

#11	Susannah Perkins
#25	Lauren Patten
#13	Jenna Dioguardi
#46	Tedra Millan
#2	Sarah Mezzanotte
#7	Brenna Coates
#14	Samia Finnerty
#8	Midori Francis
#00	Lizzy Jutila
SOCCER MOM	Mia Barron

The Wolves was remounted on December 5, 2016 by special arrangement with Scott Rudin and Eli Bush. The producers, location, director, and design remained the same. The Production Stage Manager was Amanda Spooner. The cast remained the same, except:

SOCCER MOM	Kate Arrington

Originally presented by New York Stage and Film and Vassar in the Powerhouse Season, Summer 2016. Playwrights Horizons Theater School produced a workshop of *The Wolves* in 2015 in association with Clubbed Thumb, where the play had been developed previously.

Produced by Lincoln Center Theater, New York City, 2017.

Characters

#11 Midfield. Brainy, morbid, budding elitist, thoughtful. Seventeen.

#25 Defense, Captain. Classic (ex)coach's daughter. Seventeen.

#13 Midfield. Stoner, older pot dealer brother, into her wackiness. Sixteen.

#46 Bench. New girl. Awkward, different, just wants to fit in. Sixteen.

#2 Defense. Innocent, unlucky, kind, skinny. Sixteen.

#7 Striker. Too cool for school. Sarcastic, "fuck", thick eyeliner. Almost seventeen.

#14 Midfield. #7's insecure sidekick. Just switched to contacts. Sixteen.

#8 Defense. Childlike and determined to stay that way. Sixteen.

#00 Goalie. Intense performance anxiety, perfectionist, high achiever. Seventeen.

SOCCER MOM

Setting

An indoor soccer field somewhere in suburban America. The field is AstroTurf. We only see the field: no goals, no bleachers. Fans, flourescents. There should be the sense that the field goes on forever.

Winter. Saturdays.

Note

Each scene is a warm-up for a game. The warm-up is a series of exactly timed stretches and exercises: squats, jumping jacks, quads, hamstrings, butterfly, etc. The team executes it wordlessly, in perfect unison and with military precision.

Over the course of the play, #46 learns the warm-up.

Speed

The play should take 90 minutes

Week One—The Cambodian

nine girls in uniform stretch in a circle on an astroturf indoor soccer field
they do the same stretch at the same time for the same amount of time

#11
but it's like
he's old

#25
he murdered 1000s of people

#13
literally 100s of 1000s

> #2
> *(to #8, quiet)*
> have you played with it before?

#11
yeah but did you see the photo?

> #8
> what?

#46
what photo

#13
the photo

> #2
> nothing

#25
oh yeah the photo

> #14°
> what'd you say?

> #2
> *(a little louder)*
> have you played with it before

°#14 has a cold this week

#7
like yeah of course we have
We're Women
that's like what we do

#11
yeah he's like 90 years old
and like has the old person eyes

#2
has it been a problem?

#11
and all these wrinkles
and like gave testimony on Skype from his hospital bed

#7
like has blood run down my legs?

#14 laughs hysterically

#25
I don't think they have Skype in Cambodia

#13
that is like so

#25
what

#13
like so bad

#8
it's really no big deal

#13
like you can't say that
cause it's like

#11
yeah

#13
insensitive

#8
seriously

#25
no
no it's not
it's not insensitive

#11
they definitely have Skype in Cambodia

#25
the internet isn't the internet everywhere you guys

#46
are you talking about Cambodia?

> #2
> (*terrified*)
> what if like my pad falls out?

#13
that's the stupidest shit

#11
no
she's right

> #8
> omigosh

#25
yeah
(*thank you*)
it's like
like here we can look up whatever we want

> #7
> you still use those?

#25
but like in China they don't have Twitter in China

> #7
> that's like running around with a diaper or something
>
> #14
> you gotta get off of those

#11
well that's not exactly

> #14
> you want a ?
> cause I can get you one
>
> #8
> same

#2
(shakes head no)

#7
no you want it
trust me you want it

#11
I'm pretty sure they have a Twitter like platform in China

#14
(motions off)
they're just in my backpack

#2
(on the verge of tears)
no
thank you

#25
uh platform?

#8
you should like totally take one

#7
(you remember Courtney)

#2
yeah

#14
(oh Jesus Courtney)

#13
are you saying
you're on Chinese Twitter
or something?

#8
it's not so hard
you just like
pop!
I have like
special sporty ones
like the ones on tv

#7
(with the super plus)

#14
(oh my god yes)

#11
no

#7
little perv

#11
I'm not on Chinese

#2
we don't have tv

#14
hahaha
hahaha
hahaha

#11
I'm just

#8
omigosh
that's so sad!
I always forget that
about you

#11
I mean like
yeah we *should*
take our liberties for granted

#13
um

#11
what

#13
um no we should not

    #7
    wait

#13
we should like definitely not
take our liberties for granted

    #7
    what if it ran down and like

#11
I never said we should take our liberties for granted

    #7
    stained the ball

#13
um

#25
you did

    #2
    what?

    #8
    ew

#11
no
I didn't

    #14
    that would be like so epic

#11
I would never say that

    #14
    like so scary for the other team

#46
I've been to Cambodia

#7
yeah like
"score on me with my own baby blood?
I think not!"

#13
we should be like very very thankful for our liberties you know

#14
yeah ha like

#11
oh my god I like totally know and believe in that
guys you know what I

#46
(louder)
I've been to Phnom Penh

#14
"want a piece of me?
here! have a piece of my / ovary"

#11
I am like

#7
yeah like
(pause to think of joke)

#11
firmly pro-liberty

#14
totally
haha

#7
like you know
uh

#11
I just / meant like

#7

mpon bitchessss!

#14
hahaha yeahhh

#8
gross!

#14
"you got my period on your cleats fool"

#7
SUCK IT

#8
you guys are being soooo gross

#2 *abruptly stands up*
jogs away from the circle

#8
yay! she's doing it! you go girl!

#2
no I just um
I have to go to the portaparty
. . . portapotty

#14
take one
seriously
they're in my backpack in a little polka dot thing

#7
RUN BITCH RUN

#25
language

#7 *and #14 exchange an eye-roll*

#25
HUSTLE BACK
KICK-OFF'S IN TEN

#14
GUYSGUYSGUYS:
she uses pads

#13
DUDE!

#25
hey

#13
haha nasty

#25
HEY

#13
portaparty?
more like
portapartaaay

#8
(to #7)
you know she doesn't like that word

#7
I don't like your face
doesn't mean it doesn't exist

#11
really?

#7
yep

#13
weird

#8
(scolding)
you guys her family is like super religious

#11
um what does that have to do with her feminine product of choice

#13
word up

#8
I just don't think we should call her
we shouldn't use the
the b-word

#7
bitch

#14
ha biotch

#25
hey

#14
oh my god it is just like a female dog!

#13
I hear she like
she like speaks in tongues

#8
no she doesn't

#13
that's not what Kristen told me

#8
she doesn't
she goes to my step-mom's church
she's Episcopalian

#13
(speaking in tongues aka ululation)
lalalalalala

#11
I saw this documentary on Netflix
about like snake handling
have you guys heard about snake handling

#7
more like
Bitch-co-palian

#13
(tongues become more of a song)
lalalalalala

#11
all these southerners like die of snakebites
while like communing with god
it's so dark

#25
why would you watch a documentary?

#11
I dunno
it's cool stuff

#14
or like
like
E-bitch-co-palian

#7
um hello
just made that joke

#11
they have so many options on there
you should check it out

#13
lalalalalalala
lalalalalalala
lalalalalalala
lalalalalalala
lalalalalalala
lalalalalalala
lalalalalalala
lalalalalalala
lalalalalalala
lalalala

#14
ha yeah you did

#25
but for fun?
you do that for fun?

#7
shut up whore

#11
yeah
or like
on family movie night
(to #13)
would you shut up?

#14
ha ha shut it you uh
you uh

#7
make me bitch

did you say
family
mooooovie
night?

#14
. . . ok

#25
you guys do movie nights?

#14 slaps #7 in boob

#11
I don't want to talk about it

#7
OW!

#25
Ladies

#14
(to 7)
baby

#7
that hurt asshole

#14
faker baby

#7
fuck you they're really tender right now

#25
Ladies

#46
(trying to get in on the fun)
is it because you are pregnant?

long awkward pause

#8
were you guys talking about the Khmer Rouge?

#11
yeah

#8
did you read that

#11
that article yeah

#46
what article

#8
so horrible

#11
yeah

#46
guys what article

#7
(to #46)
would you shut the fuck up?

#13	#14
i thought it was *(mispronounces Khmer Rouge)*	*(to #7)*
	(hey)
#11	(hey)
no I'm pretty sure it's Khmer Rouge	(hey)

#13
oh Khmer Rouge

#7
(what)

#8
yeah Khmer Rouge

#14
(are you okay?)

#13
(British accent)
Khmer Rouge

#7 *rolls her eyes*

#11
you are such an idiot

#13
whatever
I read it and like couldn't tell

#14
what's the Khmer Rouge

#13
they're like Nazis in Cambodia

#25
but in the 70s

#11
that's not / quite

#7
/you don't know about the Khmer Rouge?

#14
no
am I supposed to?
am I supposed to know about the Khmer Rouge?

#00 stands up and looks sick and jogs off

#11
they don't teach you about Cambodia at St. Albert?

#14
um I don't think so

#11
(superior)
Oh

#7
we don't do genocide 'til senior year

#8
I am getting such a bad grade in social studies
that Armenia project killed me

#14
(to #7)
how do you know about the Khmer Rouge

#7
I don't know
it's the Khmer Rouge

#46
like Hermione right
when I was little I thought it was like "herm-ee-oh / n"

#14
/were we talking about fucking harry potter?
um no we were talking about the Khmer Rouge
the Khmer Rouge ok
who were like Asian Nazis
and killed billions of people
so like have a sense of like of like

#7
not being a dick about it

#2 jogs back on and rejoins stretch circle

#11
it was 100s of 1000s of people   #8
not billions   (did you try it?)

#14
whatever

#11
that makes a huge difference
there are only like 7 billion people on the entire planet

#14
ok

#11
it's just factually inaccurate

#14
yeah I get it I was just like making a point

#11
but it wasn't the right point

#13
cha-ching

#14
does it matter?
does it really

#11
yeah
I think it does
I mean of course it does

#25
you're the one who said you felt bad cause he was old

#13
yeah
you were like "oh they can't execute him he's 90"
when he killed 100s of 1000s of human beings

#7
but he killed all those people

#2
(*vigorously shakes no*)

#8
(omigosh you should
you should take one
or at least try it)

#2
(*awkward smile*)

#8
(they're supes
comfortable)

#2
(*awkward smile*)

#8
(pop!)

#11
no that's not what I/

#2
what's she talking about?

#13
she like pities the cambodian dude just cause he's stupid old

#2
the who?

#13
you know the guy
uh
like uh   #25
new-a   have you done social studies?
noo-o
                                           #2
#11   the article response?
I thought it was chee
or like chi   #25
or something   yeah

#13   #2
no I think it was like   oh
with an n
pretty sure it was   #25
with an n   yeah

#2
(to #11)
you feel bad for him?

#11
no I don't feel bad I just

#2
he enslaved and exterminated his own people

#8
yeah wow

#11
no guys I just think it's uh
it's
(*finding the word*) ethically complicated

#13
what's so complicated about killing 100s of 1000s of people?

#7
well it's probably pretty challenging
technically

#14	#11	#13		#8	#2
wow	um	that is gnarly man		eww	*shakes head*

#7
what
think about it

#25 *sighs*

#11
no what I meant was like
ok I do think it was horrible
obviously
he was horrible

#00 *jogs back on*
rejoins the circle

#13
IS horrible

#11
yeah ok IS horrible
but
I think it's interesting

#2
it's not interesting
it's like evil

#11
ok but
imagine if you did something horrible today
but you didn't think it was horrible

#2
but it was horrible
is the thing
it was/

#11
let me finish
it was horrible
it was an an atrocity
right?

#13
yeah
it was

#11
but YOU didn't think it was an atrocity
you thought you were like saving your country
like destroying the enemy to save your own people

#2
but the enemy WAS your own people

#25
yeah

#11
right
I know that
but like
what if
after you did that
you just like lived your life
like went to college and got a job and got married and had kids and grandkids and

#13
whoa

#11
and then
when you were 90 and like on the verge of death with like uh emphysema
that's when an INTERPOL guy knocks on your door and is like
we found you
we know what you did
and guess what?
you're going to prison
For Life

long pause as it sinks in

#46
my grandma has emphysema

no one really notices that comment

#8
prison for life?
he's only going to prison for life?

#11
yeah

#8
but he's 90
he's probably going to die soon

#11
Pol Pot's already dead
most of 'em the big ones already dead

#13
freaky deeky

#2
didn't he Skype into court from his hospital bed

#11
yeah that's right
he's super sick

#2
so he might only serve a year in prison
for doing a genocide?

#11
yeah

#7
that is so fucked

whistle blows
everyone looks offstage

#25
alright
let's go let's go

the girls start to stand and get ready

#8
who are we playing again?

#25
the Hornets

#8
right

#13
those guys blow

#11
remember Las Vegas Showcase last year?

#00 smiles

#7
this girl remembers

#00 blushes

#7
you were like
"shoot on my goal?
I think not"

#14
ha ha

#11
7-0 baby

#25
4th in our bracket

#8
and then we went to Circus Circus!
guys remember Circus Circus?
with the elephants?

#11
yeah

#2
there were elephants?

#13
look at their stupid yellow jerseys
they look like like like
school buses

#8
yeah
in the big tent

#2
. . . I don't remember any elephants

#7
yeah
fucking school buses

#14
school buses

#13
schoooool busssesssss

they laugh

#25
come on
let's get on out there
Coach is waiting

general eyeroll

#14
Coach couldn't give a shit if we paid him

#7
oh that's right
we do

#11
he's like so hung-over
it's embarrassing

#2
he is?

#11
why do you think he wears those stupid athletic sunglasses
Inside
on a Saturday Morning?

#7
maybe he's still wasted

#14
definitely

#25
(ignoring that)
hustle girls

#2
maybe he's just sleepy

#13
oh bleedy
sweet sweet little bleedy

#11
he's definitely still wasted

#7
such a joke

#14 has a coughing attack
everyone looks at her

#25
are you sick?

#14
no

#25
you sound a little

#11
yeah

#13
yeah you sound all like *(nasal sounds)*

#14
(sniffling)
I feel so good you guys

#25
I don't want you here if you're sick

#14
I am totally fine
it's just like
allergies

#25
. . . alright
get on out there
hustle

#13
right right
turf allergies

#8
is that a thing?

#7
you better not get me sick before my birthday

#14
um I am so not sick

#14 and #7 jog off

#13
(to #2)
btdubs I think we've synced

#2
excuse me?

#13
I mean
we've like
our bodies bleed together

#8
ewwww

#11
gross

#13
you bleed I bleed
catch my drift

#2
(horrified and small)
cool

#11
that happened to me and my sister
our bathroom is ugh
it's like a mass grave in that trash can

#13, #2, #11, #8 run off
#25 goes up to #46 who is struggling to tie her shoes

#25
um hey

#46
hello

#25
can we talk for a sec?

#46
yes
I have lots of secs

slight pause
neither wants to acknowledge what she just said

#25
it's just uh
ok uh
try not to make jokes like that

#46
what joke?

#25
the uh
the you know

#46
(blank look)

#25
the uh pregnancy?
. . . joke?

#46
oh

#25
(nods)
yeah
yeah

#46
why?

#25
what?

#46
why can't I make a pregnancy joke?

pause

#25
I mean
we like to have fun but
you know
uh
"if you can't say something nice
don't say anything at all"?

pause

#25
(captain mode)
great
let's get on out there

#46
could I play striker?

#25
7 is striker
. . . 7 has always been striker

#46
oh

#25
it's just
we're undefeated
and we want to stay undefeated
right?
especially with the college showcase tournament coming up?

#46
. . . it's the only spot in football I haven't tried yet
I just thought
it might be easier

football??

#25
. . . it never gets easier
you just get better

. . .

#25
that's something my dad
. . .
(energetic)
I'll sub you in ASAP
kay?
now let's get out there and kick some Hornet boot-ay!

#25 jogs off
#00 is still wrapping her hands
#46 drinks her water bottle and lets it hang from her mouth lost in thought

#00
she had an abortion

#46
what?

#00 doesn't look up from her hands

#46
when?

#00
two months ago

#00 puts on her goalie gloves

#00
just cause Nuon Chea's weak
doesn't mean he shouldn't pay

#46 doesn't know how to respond to this

#00
the Cambodian?
he deserves it
even if he's weak
he deserves it

whistle

Week Two—Todos Los Niños

eight girls in uniform stretch in a circle on an astroturf indoor soccer field
they do the same stretch at the same time for the same amount of time

#2
I'm talking about Mexican children in cages

#11
not just Mexican
mostly like Guatemalan and Honduran and like   #2
all over   in cages!
all over Central America   cages!

#7*
and that's why you're selling scarves?

#2
I'm knitting them myself
well with Amnesty International
the whole club's knitting them
or I guess learning how to knit

#13
and they cost how much?

#2
25 dollars

#25
 jeez

#2
i know but it's for a good cause

---

*#7 has a cold this week

#8
I always want to call it Middle America

#14
what?

#8
Central America
I always want to call it Middle America
does anyone else do that?
Middle America?

#13
like Middle Earth?

#8
omigosh

#11
uh it's Meso America
technically

#8
Middle Earth!
omigoshhhhh

#11
and uh we are Middle America
I mean we live in Middle America

#14
what does that mean

#11
it means we're like
we're America
you know

#13
right totally like
we're not High America
we're not Low America
we're just like America America

#2
I have some in my backpack
if anyone wants to

#2
you can choose the yarn color

#7
USA
USA

#11
it's like
you know
we drive pick-up trucks and don't like cuss words

#7
the fuck is a cuss word

#8
(*sigh*)
I'd love a pick-up truck

#14
ha

#25
Hey

#13
(*to #11*)
doesn't your mom drive a Prius?

#8
like a big purple pick-up truck

#11
yeah but
you know

#13
how is Dr. Feinstein doing these days?

#11
(*wary*)
she's uh
she's great

#13
still got that smoking haircut?
and that sexy sexy bod?

#11
screw you

#13
you have got a Hot Mom
those are the cards you were dealt
and you know what
you gotta make a certain kind of peace with that

#7
um I think you meant "fuck"

#25
cut it out

#11
She is not a Hot Mom!

#13
(to #11)
that's not what Kevin says
as he jerks off to her website pic

#8
ewwww

#11
that's so wrong
he's her patient

#14
Kevin sees a shrink?

#13
uh Kevin?
hello?
Kevin?
the community college drop-out who sells pot from our basement?
he's like why shrinks were invented

#11
She's
My
Mom

#13
and He's My Brother!
that makes us like
oh man
if my brother's banging your mom
that makes me your

#11
you are such an asshole

#13
that's Auntie Asshole to you dearie

#7
that is so nasty

#25
Ladies

#8
GUYS!
omigosh you guys
does that mean we're hobbits?

#13
um
whaaaaat

#8
cause like we live in
Middle America
so like Middle Earth
so like . . . The Shire

#2
you are beyond obsessed

#8
I love that
I like love that we live in The Shire of America

#7 ACHOO

#11
that is not what Middle America

#14
bless you

#13
try telling that to the future Mrs. Samwise Gamgey

#7
thanks bitch

#8
(*dreamy*)
he's just such a good friend!
you know?

#7
jesus

#13
(*sings* Lord of the Rings *theme*)
doo doo doo doo doo doo

#8
doo doo

#2
(*joins in*)
doo doo doo doo doo doo

#7
you guys are retarded

#8
hey
don't use the r-word

#2
yeah
not cool

#7
oh get over yourselves

#25
no really
it's really not cool

#7
jesus you guys are like a bunch of fascists
haven't you heard of like free speech
like the first fucking amendment?

#25
it's just an ugly word
and it's not the sort of word we want on the field

#7
(fuck you)

#25
what was that?

#7
nothing

#25
what?

#7
jesus nothing

pause

#11
hey where's the new girl?

pause

#14
I suppose we'll just have to like manage without her

titters

#25
girls

slight pause

#8
who are we playing again?

#25
Fusion

they all look off to the other team warming up

#13
are they any good?

#25
they're ok
great goalie

#14
oh right
The Wall

#11
hey we've got a great goalie right here

#13
ow ow ow

#13 grabs #00's shoulders and she grimaces

#8
she's so huge
just look at her

#7
Christine Fucking Kratzer

#14
you think she lifts?

#11
she has to
to get that kind of muscle def

#2
I should lift more

#13
um what?
why?

#2
nobody sees me on the field and is like "uh oh"

#13
you could like get a facial tattoo
like a full-on facial tattoo

#14
yeah but you're so skinny

#2
no I'm not

#8
omigosh you so totally are

#11
yeah

#2
no I'm not I'm really not you guys

#25
if you want to bulk up maybe you should try lifting

#7
and like eating more protein

#2
I eat plenty of protein
I like basically live on peanut butter and cheese!
(deeply frustrated) ECH

#8
hey it's ok
I don't have any upper body strength either

#2
I just can't stop thinking about it

#8
really?

#2
all those Mexican kids in cages!

#11
they're not just / Mexican

#2
there's so many of them
and they're all stuck in these camps

#13
that sounds ok

#2
no like not fun camps
really horrible camps
and some of them are like Travis's age!

#8
that's super sad
I like didn't know about this at all

#2
I just really hope someone's reading to them
five to six is a really important age
especially for ESL

#8
I love reading to Patrick
it's sooo fun
I get to do all the voices
like "here comes grumpy Mr. Platypus"

#2
in my youth ministry we tutor first graders
at Jessie Beck
they're all ESL kids
and the later they come over the / harder it is

#8
ohhh
hahaha
omigosh
I thought you were
talking about biceps!
hahaha

#13
los niños!
todos los niños!
ay mamacita los pobrecitos

#11
you know you're being racist

#13
que?

#11
like super racist

#13
lo siento
tia mia
pero no hablo tu lengua estupida

#11
it's idioma? / actually?

#7
ARE YOU GUYS FUCKING BRAIN DEAD?
they have Nowhere to go
no like Legal Status
I mean they're just going to be like Deported
back to their Families who Sent them here
so they could like Have a Better Life
and like not live in a fucking War Zone with like fucking Drug Lords
but now if they like IF they even make it across the fucking Border
they're stuck
in like basically Prisons in like Arizona
and being used as like as like FUCKING POLITICAL PROPS!

#13
. . . whoa man

#2
. . . what are you saying

#7
so they have much bigger fucking problems than
than fucking
than fucking ESL BEDTIME STORIES

#14
I didn't know you cared about this stuff

#7
my dad's firm
does like a lot of immigration stuff
pro bono stuff
he's so pissed

#2
we're pissed too!
we're super pissed!
that's why we're knitting scarves!

#8
but like
didn't it take you a while to learn English?

#7
me?

#8
(to #14)
no no you

#14
. . . um what do / you

#8
like cause your family came over when you were four?
didn't it take you a while?

#14
um no
I already spoke English

#8
oh! ok
I guess that's why you don't have a Mexican uh

#14
. . . I'm Armenian

#8
oh!
. . . cool
that's so cool

#13
dude!

#11
we just learned all about Armenia

#14
yeah
I'm uh
I'm Armenian

#8
then why are you always going to Mexico with your family?

#14
um for vacation?

#8
ohhhh

#2
her dad's Armenian

#11
seriously?

#14
yeah my dad's Armenian
my mom's American
they were living in London when they had me

#13
ay yay yay chica

#8
super cool

#11
do you have double citizenship
I want double citizenship
. . . dual

#25
that's so cool

#2
I knew that

#13
ello, guvnor!
the loo! the lorry!
the. . . LON-DON!

#8
wait shouldn't you have like an English accent then?

#7
YOU GUYS ARE RETARDED

#13
whoa man

#25
would you watch that language

#7
oh yeah?
or WHAT?

#25
or I'll tell Coach

#7
oh no!
the dumbass who works at Best Buy?
see how many fucks I give

#25
that's it
I'm warning you

#7
fuck
you

#25
you're running laps

#7
I HATE YOU
I HATE YOU
I
HATE
YOU

#7 storms off

#25
well
we'll uh
we'll see if she starts this game huh

pause

#13
(shouldn't you uh)

#14 . . . (yeah)
(yeah)

#14 jogs off after #7
#46 walks in wearing a puffy coat over street clothes and odd snow boots

#13
there go our Lady Crusaders

#11
St. Albert has like the most Catholic team name

#13
could be like the Lady Jesus
the Lady Jesus's
the Lady Jesi?

#8
guys I totally thought she was Mexican

#2
I knew she was Armenian
her nana used to make these Armenian pastries

#8
i forgot you guys used to be like best best friends

#2
yeah
she taught me how to knit when I was like 7
we'd knit and watch Power Rangers in her den

#13
GO GO POWER RANGERS!

#8
guys I feel horrible
was that horrible?

#11
(to 8)
it's not a bad thing
to be Mexican

#8
no I know I just

#46
I've been to Armenia

slight pause where they notice her

#13
viva la Mexica!

#11
it's viva Mexico

#13
viva Mexico!

#11
you are THE MOST annoying

#25
oh!
hey!
you made it!

#46
sorry
my bus

#13
(her bus?)

#25
. . . that's great!
get changed and get back out here
alright?

#46 *just stands there*

#25
what's up?

#46
the locker room's closed

#25
oh yeah uh
hm

#11
portapotty?

#46 *looks uncomfortable*

#25
yeah I guess you should use the portapotty
sorry

#46 *stands for a sec and then exits*

#13
she takes the bus?

#11
she told me she has to take like 3 buses to get here

#8
wow

#13
doesn't she live in like the hills?

#8
really?

#13
yeah I heard she lives in the hills in this like yogurt thing with her mom

#2
she lives in a yogurt?

#46 reenters
she forgot her backpack

#46
. . . backpack

#46 grabs it and exits

#13
I can't imagine being homeschooled

#25
yeah

#11
totally

#8
yeah
so weird

#13
she doesn't even have a school season
you know

#8
and it's like so weird she just joined our team

#11
nobody does that

#8
I mean we've been playing together forever

#2
remember The Blossoms

#13
(to #25)
oh man when your dad was our coach

#11
Coach Frank

#13
good ol' Screamy Screamy Coach Frank

#25
(embarrassed)
yeah
yeah

#11
can always tell when Frank's around

#13
first one in the lawn chair
first one out of the lawn chair
punching a ref in the face

#25
that was two years ago

#2
he just cares a lot

#8
but like
she's only now playing indoor?
like—really?

#25
I mean
she's pretty good
for having never played before

#13
wait
whaaaaat

#2
seriously?

#8
she's never played before??
like ever?

#25
that's what she said on her registration form

#8
omigosh

#11
you get to see the registration forms?

#13
like on a team?
or like indoor?
or like at all?

#25
I don't know

#11
like all the registration forms?

#25
yeah uh
Coach showed them to me

#8
wow
then she's like a
wow she's like a prodigy

#13
yeah dude

#25
I asked her if she wanted to play travel team
and she was like
"what's travel team"

13
NO

#8
omigosh

#11
they just moved here you know

#25
and she called it "football"

#11
what??

#13
like as a joke?

#25
yeah she called soccer "football"
and positions "spots"

#13
as a joke
right?

#25
I don't think so

#8
that is like so sad

#13
truth to power?
she's pretty stinky

#8
omigosh I know

#11
she doesn't shave

#8
like anywhere?

#13
WHOA is she even like American?

#2
guys should we really be

#13
what

#2
. . . like behind her back
I don't feel comfortable with uh
you know

pause

#13
uh
ok

#00 stands up and runs off looking sick

#25
hope they finish construction soon

#8
yeah that portapotty is like so disgusting

#13
yeah last week
after the game
someone was in there for like EVER
and I really had to go
but like finally finally they open the door
and it was
you won't even believe it:
Louise

#11
no

#13
yeah
oh yeah
Lou-ise

#25
Louise Peterson?

#13
yep
yep

#8
what was she doing here?

#13
and of course I get in there and she took like the HUGEST dump

#8
ewwww

#11
did not need to know that

#25
I think she's sort of cool

13
. . .. dude
what??

#2
who's Louise Peterson?

#11
oh she's that new girl
super punk

#8
she sang in that coffee house?
and like licked the microphone?

#2
oh
her

#13
you think she's sorta cool?

#8
she is so WEIRD

#25
I don't know

#8
she smells like cigarettes

#13
she has such a creepy laugh
she sits behind me in precalc
and does this weird little creepy laugh

#8
and her hair
she has weird hair
it's like
pokey

#13
"he he he"
"he he he"

#11
ha ha

#25
yeah

#13
"he he he"

#25
ok ok

*#46 walks in in uniform
sits down*

#25
I just think she's sorta different

#13
"oh Louise
you're just
sorta
different"

#13 fake makes out with Louise

#8
ewww

#25
(blushing)
guys that's
you're being so immature
she's really smart
we're in the same AP English / class and

#46
(loudly, to #2)
/I think you meant yurt

#2
(very polite)
. . . excuse me?

#46
you said yogurt
I think you meant yurt
I live in a yurt with my mom

#2
. . . oh

#46
you can't really live in a yogurt

uneasy laughter

#46
hey I uh just saw the uh
(can't remember her name)
uh goalie? outside? and i think she's/

#11
vomiting?

#13
(makes the sound)

#8
ewwwww

#13
(makes the sound on #8)

#8
stop stop stop

#46
(confused that they know this is happening)
yeah uh
is she alright?

#25
she vomits before every game

#13
and she stops talking
like totally clams up

#11
it's a nervous condition

#8
it's like disgusting is what it is

#11
she's like super high functioning

#13
basically a genius

#25
she has a 4.9
and edits the *East Gazette*

#11
I'm a columnist

#2
she has a 4.9?

#8
and plays the saxophone in State Youth Orchestra

#25
and leads Model UN

#11
but crippling SAD

#2
she's not very sad

#11
no no

#11
SAD
S.A.D.
Social Anxiety Disorder

#46
oh
well that explains that I guess

light laughter
awkward silence

#46
i think there's a bird in the air dome

they all look up

#25
that happens sometimes

#11
what I want to know is how they get in

#13
dude I do not want to be in here
if there's a hole in the air dome

#11
I think we'd be ok

#8
there's a hole in the air dome?

#13
nuh uh have you like SEEN a balloon pop before

#11
um I think it's more complicated than that

awkward silence

#46
. . . you can tell by the rusty flanks

#2
where?

#46
right there
on top of the ventilation unit

#2
where?

#46
(pointing) there

#2
oh!
pretty

#46
I think it's a tufted
titmouse

awkward-er silence

#46
(trying to gossip)
hey so uh who knows about 7's abortion?

pause

#13
wow

pause

#25
that's uh
we don't say stuff like that

#46
(totally mortified)
cool

#13
I thought she just took Plan B

#8
that's not what I heard

#13
no I'm pretty sure it was just Plan B

#11
maybe she had an abortion
AND took Plan B

#25
come on guys

#11
what
it's a possibility
it's a definite possibility

#13
are we talking about two months ago?
when Dan came home for Thanksgiving?

#25
yeah

#13
no guys that was definitely Plan B

#2
how do you know

#13
Miss Armenia told me
. . . guys we cannot go around telling people she got an abortion

#2
what's Plan B?

#14 and #7 jog in
#14 holds something behind her back

#2
guys? what's / Plan

#25	#13	#11
look who's back!	yo yo!	hey guys!

#8
OH
hi
hello

#7
were you guys talking about us or something?

#13		
uh	#8	#11
nope	hahahaha	there's a bird in the air dome
	hahahaha	

#7
what-ever
big news guys:

#14
my mom brought orange slices

she tosses orange slices into the group
they stop stretching and descend on the Ziploc bag

#13
orange slices! dude!

#8
omigosh

#2
your mom's the best

#7
(sarcastic)
she's like the Total Best

#14
ha totally

#8
orange slices!
that's so so fun!
guys remember when

#11
yes we all remember orange slices

#13
oh god
they're delicious

#25
don't eat too many ladies
no side cramps out there

#13
hey guys look

#13 puts orange rind into teeth and smiles

#8
guys we used to do this all the time! oh my god

#8 puts orange rind into teeth and smiles

#11
ha that rules

#11 puts orange rind into teeth and smiles

#8
(orange slice in mouth)
(you gotta do it)

#8 holds an orange rind out to #2

#2
oh
um

#8
(come on come on)

#2 hesitates for a sec then puts orange rind into teeth and smiles
she looks super stressed out
#7 and #14 join in

#13
(my dudes I've got braces)

#13
(look I'm 12 years old)

#13
(I've got braces)

#11
(this tastes funny after a while)

#8
(isn't this super fun)

#7
(wow)

#14
**(haha
haha
haha)**

#25
um girls

#14
(takes out orange slice)
WAIT

we should take a picture
does anyone have their phone
mine's dead

#11
(no)

#8
(yay! picture!)

#2
(I don't have one)

#13
(in my backpack)

#7
(seriously?)

#14
what?

#2
(I'm not allowed)

#13
(takes out orange slice)
in my backpack
the tie dye one
on the bench

#7
(um why?)

#2
(nodding)
(radiation)

#14
cool

#7
(what?)

#14 jogs off to the bench

#2
(radiation)

#25
girls we should really finish

#7
(what?)

#11
**(you know
you want
to)**

#8
**(come on
for the picture)**

#2
(takes out slice)
radiation!

#11
(radiation?)

#25 puts in a slice

#13
NO THE OTHER TIE DYE ONE
THE TURQUOISE-Y ONE

#8
**(yay!
guys!
let's all pose!
let's pose like Charlie's Angels)**

*#00 jogs on and clocks the situation
she puts an orange slice in and joins*

#13
IT'S IN THE BIG POCKET
NO THE OTHER BIG
YEAH NEXT TO MY INHALER?
BINGO BANGO MY FRIEND

#14 jogs back on with iPhone

#14
kay everybody um
do something crazy

they all pose in awesome ways except #46

#25
(takes out orange slice)
hey
wanna get in the picture?

#46
(on verge of tears)
I don't get it

#25
what?

#46
why do they have orange peels in their mouths?

they all stare at her in shock with orange peels in their mouths

#25
wow
uh
just do it ok?

*#46 puts an orange in
and gets in the picture*

#14
alright

#8 and #2
LET'S POSE LIKE CHARLIE'S ANGELS

#7
um, no
let's just like do whatever

#8
(disappointed)
ok

um
look fierce

#14 takes the photo with an iPhone

#14
very cool you guys

they spit them out and crowd around the iPhone

#7   #13   #11
can I see?   did you use the filter   oranges are so good you guys

#8   #2
wait we should do a goofy one   *(cleans off her tongue)*
guys can we do a goofy one

#13
(looking at it)
very nice
want me to take one with you in it?

whistle

#25
alright that's game
let's get out there ladies!
hustle!
someone grab the slices!
                              #2
                              I'll get em   #13
#25   Fusion is going downnnntownnn
let's go let's go

#7
time to climb The Wall   #13
                                    more like *(monster voice)* DESTROY IT

#14
(to #00)
hey my ACL's acting up
can I use your wrap

#00
(*nods*)

#25
how's it feeling

#14   #11
you know   can I have some too?

#25 jogs off with #00 and #14 and #11

#8
hey do you think they play soccer?

#13
who?

#8
all the immigrant kids
do you think someone gives them like mini soccer balls?

#7
jesus christ

#8
what?
what?

#13
muy muy muy racista

#8, #7, #13 jog off
#2 picks up the orange slices and looks at #46 who looks up

#2
hey um

#46
the tufted titmouse is still there

#2
oh
cool

#46
but now I'm thinking it's more of a bushtit

#2
oh
that's good
. . . um
I just wanted to
I wanted to say
it's so nice you're trying a new sport

#46
. . . thanks

#2
I mean it must be hard
to move somewhere?
and not know anyone?
. . .
I guess what I mean is I'm
. . .
I'm sorry I said you lived in a yogurt

#46
right

#2
I think it's neat
. . . a yurt sounds pretty neat

#46 stares at her for a sec
and jogs off

#2 devours the entire bag of orange slices

whistle

Week Three—Martin Luther King Jr Day

the field is empty

maybe we can hear the sounds of the air dome
other games
parents cheering
boyfriends cheering
an aerobics class and a treadmill or two

it's still empty

#25
(running backwards)
HIGH KNEES

the whole team runs past doing high knees
a few seconds
they run past again

#25
(running backwards)
BUTT KICKS

they run past doing butt kicks
a few seconds
they run past again

#25
(running backwards)
HIGH KNEES / BUTT KICKS

they run past doing high knees / butt kicks
a few seconds
they run past again

#25
(running backwards)
GRAPEVINE

they run past doing grapevine
a few seconds
they run past again

#25
ALRIGHT COME IN
COME IN

#11*
(winded)
jesus she's working us

#7   #11
(winded)   *(coughing)*
cause we fucking lost
                                            #2
                                            (winded)
#14   are you ok?
(winded)
to fucking fusion   #11
                                            (winded)
                                            yeah totally
#13
(winded)
never again guys
never again

#25 carries a mesh bag of soccer balls
she empties it

#25
ALRIGHT ALRIGHT
LET'S HUSTLE
BIG GAME TODAY
AND IT'S NOT GOING TO WIN ITSELF

#13
Blue Storm is going downnn

#7
bitches won't know what hit em

---

*#11 and #00 have a cold in part three

#25
PARTNER UP

#14 and #7 pair up immediately

#25
I WANT TO SEE TIGHT PASSES
SOFT TOUCHES
INSIDE OUTSIDE
LEFT RIGHT
HUSTLE LADIES

>   #2
>   *(to #13)*
>   partner?

#25
I WANT US LOOKING GOOD OUT THERE TODAY

>   #13
>   *(detective-y)*
>   sure thing sweetheart

#25
(to 00)
ready?

#00 nods and puts on her gloves

>   #2
>   *(confused by reference)*
>   . . . ok

#7
(to #14)
did you bring your stuff?

#14
(innocent)
what stuff?

#7
um like a bikini?
a toothbrush?

#14
(*overplaying*)
oh oops I like totally forgot
guess I'll just have to SKINNY DIP

> #8
> god I hope we win

#7
(*with love and delight*)
you total fucking slut!

> #11
> we have to
> we have to beat them

> #8
> (*sigh of longing*)
> Miami

> #11
> they went to Epcot
> you know?
> Epcot
> in a limo
> with like discounted tickets

> #8
> its so unfair

> #11
> and our final game
> last spring
> all-district tournament
> was like SO CLOSE

> #8
> I know

> #46 *approaches them*

#46
hey um
mind if I join?

#11
oh
uh
ok
sure
sure

#13
sick headgear bra

#2 is wearing a protective headband

#11
we'll make it a triangle

#2
I hate it
my mom's making me wear it
she bought it on Amazon

#13
cause of last week

#2
yeah apparently I got another concussion or something

#13
oh mannnn
this is number?

#2
5 I think
no no
6

#13
you're like Queen of the CAT scan

#2
yeah my mom's like "thank god we have insurance now" but

#13   #25 *(to #00)*
yo!   quick hands
we should get you like a kitty tiara!

#2   #25 *(to #00)*
what?   quick hands

#13
(British accent)
"Queen of the CAT Scan"

#2   #25 *(to #00)*
oh!   there we go
that's funny

#13   #25 (to #00)
meow meow   that's more like it

#2
(not quite a british accent)
"Queen of the CAT scan"

they're both a little embarrassed about her bad accent

#13
your mom was freaking out

#2
my mom was totally freaking

#13
it was a sick header though

#2
right?

          #7
          I am so fucking pumped

#14
yeah Martin Luther King Jr Day is like totally my favorite holiday

#7
shut up asshole

#14
oh right
and it's your birthday

#7
oh right
and we're going to my dad's ski house
and that asshole won't be there
and he has like a fully stocked bar

#46
(*offstage*)
sorry

she runs across stage

#8
(*offstage*)
it's ok

#7
so shut the fuck up you ungrateful whore

#8 and #11 wait for her to bring the ball

#11
. . .
. . .
have you heard about diedinhouse.com

#8
what

#11
diedinhouse.com
it's a service
you pay them and they tell you if anyone has died in your house

#8
how do you find this stuff
that is so scary

#11
just the internet

#8
but you have to search for something like that   #25 *and* #00 *run across*
why would you search for

#11
no it was like on
like on my gmail
like an ad
or on Facebook or something
I don't know

#46 *walks back on with ball and stands behind* #8

#8
so creepy

#46
what is?

#8
OMIGOSH
omigosh
omigosh you scared me

#11
diedinhouse.com
it like tells you if someone died in your house or something

#46
someone died in my house

slight pause

#11
who

#46
I don't know
he won't tell me his name

#8
Oh
My
Gosh

#11
. . . don't you mean your yurt?

>#13
>I hear a scout's coming for Jordana today
>
>#2
>what?
>
>#13
>yep
>Jordana Frye
>
>#2
>really?
>
>#13
>yep yep
>
>#2
>crap
>. . .
>. . .
>she's so good
>
>#13
>I know

#7
OW

#14
what

#7
I forgot how much these hurt

#14
what?

#7
I just got waxed

#14
ohhh

#7
owwww

#00
ACHOO

#14
I can't believe you do that
it must be like so painful

#7
I guess

#25
are you sick?

#14
my sister says it's like bitchslapping your vagina
but with hot oil
like a hot oil bitchslap

#25
goddamit

#7
I have a pretty high pain tolerance so

#14
wait
is Dan coming this weekend?

#7
it's my birthday so like he better fucking come

#14
and you didn't invite anyone else?

#7
well Dan's bringing a friend

#14
(uncomfortable)
so it's just you and Dan
and me and like some college guy I don't know

#7
chill the fuck
kay
he's hot
we'll ski
we'll go in the Jacuzzi
Dan'll make his famous screwdrivers
it'll be crazy
kay?

#14
kay

> #8 *(offstage)*
> WAIT

#14
how hot

> #11
> so some guy died in your yurt?
> and he like haunts it?
>
> #46
> perhaps
>
> #8
> omigosh you guys I am so scared
>
> #11
> how do you know it's a spirit
> what if it's just a drafty window
>
> #46
> yurts don't have windows
>
> #8
> or like
> like a door
> do you have a door?

#25
LADIES!
COME IN!

> #11
> of course she has a door
> how else would she get inside the yurt
>
> #8
> I don't know
> I do not know

#25
COME IN!

> #8
> . . . with a spoon?

> *they giggle like only 16-year-olds can*

#25
what's so funny

> #11
> *(laughing)*
> "with a spoon"
>
> #8
> *(laughing)*
> "how else? with a spoon"

#25
Ladies

> #11
> *(laughing)*
> cause
> cause yogurt
> you know
>
> #8   #2
> *(laughing)*   when we get scholarships
> "with a spoon"   do you think they'll be full-ride?

#11
oh man
sorry

#13
uh
those are pretty rare

#7
(plus they're just a bunch of
dumb virgins)

#8
whoo

#11
phew

#2
right

#14
hahaha

#7
(or like
secret lesbians)

#8
spoon

#11
spoon

#2
right

#14
hahahaha

#46 intercepts their pass
she juggles their ball
she is amazing

#46
(sing/chants)
I live in a yogurt
my feelings don't get hurt
yogurt for breakfast
yogurt for lunch
I live in a yogurt
my feelings don't get hurt
yogurt for dinner
yogurt for brunch
I live in a yogurt
my feelings don't get hurt
yogurt for snack
yogurt for snacky snacky
I live in a yogurt
my feelings don't get hurt
yogurt for dessert
yogurt for

she drops the ball
everyone is watching

#2
wow

#46 sprints off

#11
what was that?

#13
seriously yo

#2
do you think she's ok?

#25
LADIES
. . .
just
. . .
team work makes the dream work
you know?

#25 jogs off

#25
(off-stage)
GODDAMMIT KEEP PASSING

pause

#13
you guys she sounds exactly like

#8
oh my gosh

#7
"mark your man goddammit"

#14
"if you let another goddamn ball in"

#11
"that's it goddammit we're running laps"

#13
wow wow wow

#14
that was interesting

#8
so weird
but so good at that

#7
if only she could play like center whatever

#13
Frankie Jr.
here in da flesh

#00
"I live in a yogurt"

everyone stares at her

#00
. . . it's catchy

#00 runs off to vomit

#8
can I just say
I just don't get what the big deal is about like self-knowledge

#11
. . . what?

#8
like
what's the big deal
there are so many other things to know about
why waste time knowing about yourself

#7
. . . where is this coming from?

#8
oh
I went over to Chris's house
and he was like
all moody and talking about self-knowledge

#13
total downer

#14
he's cute   #2
                                       in like a scary way

#8
yeah
I don't know
he like made fun of my calf muscles
and tried to stick his hand down my shirt

#7
cool

#8
um not really

pause

#7
let's do the spiderweb?

#2
yay!

#8
ooh I love the spiderweb

they do the spider web
it's a complicated interwoven passing drill
it's pretty impressive actually

#2
did you guys hear a scout's coming?

#11
really?

#13
for Jordana Frye

#7
shit

#14
from where?

#13
I mean I think she's getting scouted by like everyone
but I think Santa Barbara

#13
righteous

#14
yeah

#2
Santa Barbara?
you didn't tell me that

#8
but the showcase tournament isn't until next week

#13
i know they must just want like early dibs you know

#11
is that even legal? like NCAA approved legal?

#8
have you guys emailed coaches yet?
I get so nervous I never know how to start it

#7
um "dear coach"

#8
yeah but like I don't know
it just makes me nervous
what if there's like a spelling error or I say the wrong thing
or like the wrong tone

#13
you gotta chill my man

#11
wait how'd you hear that?

#13
what?

#11
about the scout?

#13
oh uh
dunno
guess Coach told me

#7
shit

#14
that's like the best team

#11
Coach?

#13
yep

#8
wait you mean like Coach Neil?
like Neil Neil?

#14
the creep who asked us to scrimmage in our sports bras?

#8
ew

#2
I hated that

#7
he's totally hungover again

#2
he is?

they all look off

#11
thus Coach Frankie Jr.

#7
which is total bullshit

#2
you guys she's doing her best

#7
we're paying out the ass for a coach

#11
our parents are paying out the ass for a coach

#7
still a fucking rip-off
Tony would never do this to boy's U-17 indoor

#8
I can't believe they got Coach Mikhail

#2
he played in Croatia right?
like on a pro team?

#11
I thought Czech Republic

#8
he is so scary

#13
I think he killed a man once
in like . . . *(scary voice)* the 80s

#14
i think he's sorta sexy

#8
he's like 45!!!!

#14	#8
so's Jude Law	so's my dad

#7
we should get fucking Coach Mikhail!
not this washed-up pudgeball who spends games at the vending machine

#13
hey
he really wanted that pop-tart

#7
it's like
it's like sexist
that's what this is
sexist

#2
c'mon it's just indoor

#7
just indoor?
we're juniors
this spring is what counts if we wanna play college

#2
I know I know but like
you know

#7
no
I don't fucking know

#00 comes back and does private goalie drills but she's listening

#8
wow you are such a feminist

#7
what?
no
it's not about
I'm just like
it's just like fucked up you know?

#11
I'm a feminist
what's wrong with being a feminist

#14
guys look

they watch him

#14
he literally fell asleep

#11
I just can't believe that Neil is in the Army

#8
really?

#2
I thought he worked at like RadioShack

#13
Best Buy yo

#11
he's National Guard
remember his stupid story about the humvee

#8
oh yeah didn't he like go to Iraq?

#13
Afghanistan

#7
if he's America's best
America is sorely fucked

#11
guys what if Neil did like Abu Ghraib shit?

#8
Abu what?

#11
oh come on you know about Abu Ghraib

#8
um no

#11
like torture in prison

#2
in Afghanistan

#7
no like Iraq

#11
yeah definitely Iraq

#14
. . . definitely

#7
those pictures of the guys with bags over their head
like naked standing on boxes

#8
ugh

#2
we saw pictures in Amnesty International

#11
I heard they'd like
the like female guards would like
would like you know

#8
like what

#11
like *(arouse them)*

#2
what?

#11
(nods)
like take off their shirts
and you know

#14
I heard about that

#8
ew with like terrorists?

#2
why?

#13
guys Neil did not torture terrorists with his titties

#7
oh yeah?
how would you know?

#8
I miss Coach Patrick

#2
yeah

#14
I know

#8
I love Coach Patrick

#11
can't believe he's in Idaho

#2
we should send him a card or something

#14
we should like text him that orange slice pic
as like a "get-well" thing

#7
for him or for his mom?

#8
it's so amazing he moved home

#14
what's wrong with her again?

#11
I think she has terminal breast cancer?

#14
oh right

#13
yeah
like stage 4 right?

#8
I hope he's back by March
I do not want coach creep for travel team

#13
you realize that means you want his mom to croak

#8
what??

#13
cause that's the only way he's moving back
is if his mom you know

#2
that's an awful thing to say

#13
I mean
would you rather have Coach Patrick's mom die from breast cancer OR
have Neil for travel team?

#8
. . . um

#13
are you hesitating??

#8   #7
no I mean   wow

#8   #14   #11
no   WOW   that's nuts
guys!

#7
that is some intense shit

#13
she's just a sweet old lady with one titty!

                                #11
#8   what's with you and titties today?
guys come on
I just like hate Coach Neil

#7
hate him enough to kill Coach Patrick's mom?

#8
(*getting upset*)
oh my gosh you guys

#2
guys?

#11
yeah but you don't NOT want to kill his mother

#2
hey you guys?

#7 exactly

#13
girl wants mommy to die of the big C

#8
(*on verge of tears*)
I DO NOT!!!
Take it back!!!

#13
what?

#8
you're not allowed to say that!!
take it back!!

#13
ok!!
jesus!
I take it back!!
it is taken back!!

#8 is super upset

#13
oh
shit
your mom   #11
I forgot   yeah
I'm sorry   sorry
. . . shit   #7
                    #14   yikes
                    yeah

#8
(*still really upset*)
. . . it's fine

#2
are you ok?

#8
I'm great

awkward pause

#7
soooo
who has plans for the three day weekend?

#11
homework
lots and lots of homework

#2
I'm doing a day of service at Wingfield Park
you guys should come!

#11
how do you have time?

#2
already finished my paper on Rwanda

#11 seriously?
you suck

#8
(*chipper*)
hey isn't it almost someone's birthday??

#11
(*to #7*)
right! January 19

#8
birthstone: garnet

#13
(*to #8*)
hey
that was like
major FOOT in MOUTH

#2
happy birthday!

#7
what?

#8
remember? the birthstone club?

#11
party tonight or Sunday?

#2
yeah when's it/

#7
oh I'm actually just like
hanging with Dan
at my dad's ski house

#8
you're not having a party this year?

#11
oh

#7
nah
too old for like slumber parties

#2
but you always have a slumber party

#7
yeah
yeah

#8
WELL
my stepmom said I could have some people over
so if anyone wants to sleep over Sunday?
we can like watch a movie?

#11
definitely
free me from the tyranny of Sunday night dinners

#00
(nods)

#2
I'll ask my mom

#13
want me to bring my laptop??

#8
(to #14)
omigosh
will you bring your iPad
so we can watch *Game of Thrones*??

#14
um
I'm like going out of town actually?
with my family
to like visit my cousins

#8
oh!
the Armenians?

#8
does anyone else have HBOGO?

#11
we could ask Stephanie
are you inviting Stephanie?

#8
yeah

#13
hey
I have HBOGO

#8
(sorta displeased)
cool

#13
coolio!
I'll bring my laptop

#11
also guys:
guess what our fine captain is up to this weekend

#14
. . . the Americans

        #2
        that sounds nice

#13
I have HBOGO!!

#7
taking a fucking chill pill

laughter

#11
hanging out with—
drumroll please—
Louise

#7
who?

#14
yeah who?

#13
no

#8
weird new girl at our school
she licked the microphone

#11
yes

#13
Louise Peterson?

#7
she did what?

#25 and #46 jog back in
#25 is so stressed

#14
yeah who?

#25
ALRIGHT
LET'S CIRCLE UP

they circle up

#8
omigosh why

#11
shhhh

#13
shut up

#8
(wait why is she hanging out with Louise)

#11
(exactly)

#25
OK LADIES
So

Big Game Today
Great practice for the college showcase tournament / next week

#7
/we're not going to stretch?

#25
no time

#7
um hello that is like so fucking dangerous

#14
yeah

#11
yeah the doctor said

#25
we don't have time ok
WE DON'T HAVE TIME

#7 and #14 exchange a look

#25
ok you know what?
Everyone stretch
right now
yeah

they do

#25
yeah
ok
great
So
Let's talk about last week
we lost last week
Right
Yeah
We Did

#7
(is this like her motivational speech?)

to a team that was worse than we were
Why?
Cause we weren't listening to each other

#14
(oy)

(to #7 and #14) I'm sorry Am I Interrupting??

#7
nope

#25
Good
Now
This week
We're playing a good team

#13
BLUE STORMMMMM

#25
but we've beat them before

#11
like 5 years ago

#13
or as I like to call it
Phase Training Bra

#25
OK
So
We know they're good and sure
they are
they're really good
they went to nationals last year right? but are we scared?

#7 and #14 roll their eyes

#25
I said
Are We Scared?

#2
(super loud)
NO!!!

#25
that's right
we're not scared
We're Ready to Play

#2
WE'RE READY!!

#25
Cause This isn't about Last Year's Nationals
This isn't about Next Year's Nationals
This is about Right Here
Right Now
in City Sports Dome
so
. . . expect lots of shots on goal
which means mark your man
watch for breakaways
we're gonna play 2-2-1
I want 8 and me on D
14 and 11 in midfield
(to #14 and #8)
but I want you guys to hang back play safe

#14   #11
gotcha   yep

#25
and 46 as striker

#7
. . . what?

#25
(ignoring)
7 and 13 we'll sub you in fast
it's going to be a running game
so we'll be switching it / up constantly

#7
the fuck are you talking about

#25
they're really going to run us out there
and everybody watch / for Jordana

#7
we're playing the best team in the league

#7
in the fucking district
and you bench me?

#25
hey this is all coming from Coach

#7
give it a fucking break

#25
language

#7
she can't even kick the fucking ball straight!

#25
HEY
we're a team
you wanna play?
you play With Us
All of Us
kay?

#7
(salutes)
Yes Sir

slight pause

#13
did you hear a scout's coming today

#8
yeah UC Santa Barbara

#11
for Jordana

#25
UC Santa Barbara?

#13
yep yep

#25
but tournament is a week away

#13
I know
they're just like
early bird gets the worm ya know

slight pause

#25
Ladies
get that outta your head
and leave it off the field
Alright?

#2
YEAH!

#25
Now Let's Push Ourselves Today
Push Further Than You Think You Can
And Keep On Pushing
Cause I don't know about you
But Goddamit I Want to Win

#8
kick some Blue Storm booty!

#13
ow ow!

#2
let's freaking kill em!

#11
let's do it

whistle

#25
that's kick-off
let's cheer and get out there

they huddle up real tight heads down
we hear whispers of "we are the wolves" but then

#8
AHHHHHH!

#8 breaks the circle

#14
jesus

#8
omigosh there's blood all over my jersey!!

#11
(to #2)
your nose is bleeding

#2
what?

#2 has a nosebleed

#14
jesus it's like gushing blood

#2 touches it and looks at her finger

whistle

Week Four—The Cambodian II

seven girls in uniform run in from the cold
they're sweaty and pumped up and dusted with snow

#8*
omigosh it is freezing out there!!!

#13*
whoo yeah

#13 puffs on inhaler

#2*
I can't feel my ears

#11
it's cold as shit

#14
colder than a witch's tit

#2
can you guys feel your ears?

#8
what's the point of doing a warm-up run
outside
when it's snowing?

#13
(exhales inhaler)
um
what?

#25*
keeps the blood pumping

#14
what?

#11
I mean it's also a cool-down
technically

#13
a witch's tit?

#2
how many more today?
I feel icky

#13
um
yeah?

---

*#8 and #25 and #2 and #13 have a cold this week

#8
one more

#13
are witch's tits
like
particularly cold?

#11
at least

#25
ALRIGHT LADIES
great game

#8
woo woo!

#13
we were on fi-yahhhhhh

#11
SHE was on fire

#25
yeah yeah we looked good today
 but we've got another one in 30
so let's hydrate
and circle up

#13
college showcase tour-na-MENT

they circle up and start the warm-up

#13
shit guys
shit
can I just say
that was
So Sick

#11
completely nuts

#2
I've never seen anyone play like that
even in like the World Cup

#8
omigosh she's so good

#14
who knew?

#11
I mean she was pretty good last week

#25
that bicycle kick

#13
not like this man

#14
she's been holding out on us

                    #8
                    and like in front of all of these scouts??

#2
wait where'd she go?

#7 walks in on crutches with a boot
she's in street clothes with a team hoodie and a Frappuccino
she has a ski goggle tan and so does #14

#7
what's up sluts

#14 rolls her eyes

#8
omigosh hey!   #2
                    hi!

                            #11
                            heard you cheering out there

                                        #13
                                        "fucking kill em"

#7
haha yeah
you guys were fucking great

#2
thanks!

#7
nice helmet

#2 is wearing even bigger headgear

#2
(blushes)
my mom

                            #11
                            cause of the nosebleeds?

#13
sweet ride dude

                            #2 nods

#7
fuck you
my armpits are killing me

#13
ha ha

#8
how's it feeling?

#7
you know
like super shitty

#11
oof that sucks   #8
                                                  (blows air through lips)

#7
but I have a pretty high pain tolerance so

#14 rolls her eyes

#25
what'd the doctor say?

#7
torn ACL

collective sigh

#13
shit dude

#11
aw man
it didn't look that bad on the field

#8
I thought it was a sprain at most

#7
yeah
well
guess not

#2
what a lousy birthday present

#7
haha yeah

#13
"happy 17!
here, have a bum knee for the REST OF YOUR / ADULT LIFE"

#11
/shhhh

#2
do you need surgery?

#7
looks like it

collective sigh

#11
it's not so bad
I was back on the field in a couple of months

#7
yeah

#8
but that was what
like U-14

#11
U-12
but still

#2
(to #14)
and it only took you like ten weeks
last season
right?

#14
(to #2)
yeah
but it was a less serious injury

#7
lucky bitch

#14
(*biting*)
yep
and I took really good care of it

slight pause

#7
yeah
it pretty much fucking blows
but they say maybe I'll be back in time for travel team

#2
this spring?
that's / great

#7
no
uh
fall

#2
oh

slight pause where they all feel bad

#7
maybe I can make an ID camp though

#8
cool!   #2
cool   that's so great   #13
                                          rad man

#7
yeah the Ohio one's not till August
and they're in my top ten

#11
great program at Ohio

#13
for sure

#7
yeah
as long as I rehab fast
you know

#2
totally

#13
fingers crossed man

#25
well thanks for coming out today

#7
got nothing else to do with my fucking Saturdays

laughter

#7
when's the next game?

#25
thirty minutes or so

#7
the Diablos?

#11
that's tomorrow I think

#25
tomorrow
9 am

#2
we're playing Xtreme Xplosion

#13
ack!
9 am?
that's like my primo REM cycle

#7
oh
you'll fucking destroy them

#11
hope so   #25
                           let's not get cocky

#7
strong on D but terrible shots

#25
yeah really strong D

#13
it was a pretty sweet side tackle

#7
thanks

#25
you shouldn't have kept playing on it
after that

#7
whatever
pain is a state of mind
you know

#14 rolls her eyes

#25
ok but I told you
it could have prevented surgery

#7
and I told you we should have stretched
but
can't win em all I guess

pause

#7
but we beat em!
we beat Blue Storm!
next stop nationals!

#13
"I'm in Miami bitch"

#8
(*sigh*)
Miami
oh my gosh do I want to go to Miami

#11
the look on Jordana Frye's face when the ref blew the whistle

#13
ah ha ha ha

#11
priceless

#2
it felt good

#7
hell yeah it felt good

#25
it's just indoor
doesn't count / for

#7
whatever
it's not ECNL play
but still
it fucking rocked

#14
(*pointed to #7*)
hey did you see that bicycle kick?

#8
omigosh

#13
so rad
so super rad

#11
she's a beast

#7
(*diffident*)
I guess

#14
who knew she'd be such a great striker?
right?

#8
omigosh I know
she scored like five goals!!
who does that??

#7
ok but their goalie was a total joke

#14
I hate to say it
but she's like
totally giving you a run for your money

#7
ha thanks

#14
I mean have you ever scored with a bicycle kick?

#7
I mean I can do them

#14
no you can't

#7
um yes I fucking can

#14
how come I've never seen it

#7
I do it at home
when I practice at home

#14
I bet it's like on your stupid fucking trampoline

#7
uh
no

#14
you're a fucking liar
it's on the trampoline

#7
um chill the fuck out

#14
ANYONE can do it on the fucking trampoline

#7
I can DO a fucking bicycle kick

#14
then PROVE IT you CUNT

a shocked pause from all
#46 walks in
she's happier than we've ever seen her

#46
hi guys!
great game right?
(to #7)
oh! hey!
/you made it!

#7
(to #14)
/what the fuck is wrong with you

#14
nothing

#7
uh ok

#14
I just don't have time for liars anymore
you know?

#25
HEY
I don't know what's going on but/

#7   #46
/oh fuck you   *(to #25)* um
you're not our coach
and you're a shitty / captain

#25
/and you're not playing this game
so I suggest you get off the field

#14
yeah
get off the fucking / field

#7
/you're such a prude

#14   #46
am not   um Captain

#7
that's not what Brendan said

#14
shut up

#7
it was just a fucking b /lowjob

#14   #46
(panicked)   um
shut up   uh
SHUT UP   Captain?
                                             I think Coach wants to see you

all look offstage

#2
who's that guy with Coach?

#8
I saw him on the sidelines
taking notes

#13
wait is he

#25
hydrate ladies hydrate

#25 jogs off
they all keep staring

#11
guys
he's wearing a suit

silence

they watch as #25 talks to Coach and the man in the suit

#00
shit

#25 jogs back on

#13
from what school?
did he say?

#8
Santa Barbara?
was it Santa Barbara?

#2
I bet Stanford

#11
maybe Bucknell
I invited Bucknell

#25
ladies ladies
Coach wants to see #14, #46, and #00

loaded pause

#25
go on
hustle

#14
kay

#14 and #46 and #00 jog off
#46 does a weird wave

slight pause

#7
fuck

#25
hey

#13
he's a scout
right
he has to be a scout

#25
I don't know

#7
bullshit

#25
I don't know

#7
you just shook his hand!

#11
his clipboard says Texas A & M
so I'm guessing he's from Texas A & M

pause

#7
shoulda been out there

#25
shoulda stopped playing when I told you to

#7
shoulda stretched before I played
. . . fuck

#8
. . . maybe they'll just call us over in small groups
so we can like meet him individually?

#13
sure
sure
maybe my face will turn into a walrus face

#8
(to #13)
quit it

#13 *makes a walrus face*

#2
do you guys think I played ok today?

#13 *does a vulgar walrus*

#25
you did
we all did

#8
I said quit it

#7
you were great

#11
you did miss that shot

#2
which shot?

#11
my corner kick

#2
it was too high
I couldn't get to it

#11
no it wasn't
maybe if you weren't so scared of getting another concussion

#2
it was too high

#25
hey
we all played like champs today

they all look off

#7
I've been playing for like 13 years
and she just fucking picked it up

#11
yeah
this is her first season
like ever

#8
that's like so impossible

#7
there's no fucking way

#25
ladies

#11
where'd she even move from again?

#13
she never told us
dude she never told us

#8
I bet she like played travel
or like O.D.P.
and just isn't saying

#7
you don't learn to play like that
in just a couple weeks of indoor

#13
she totally played O.D.P.

#2
(upset)
and she's SO STINKY!

#8
(to #25)
I mean I just like can't believe he didn't want you

#25
what?

#8
I mean I can't believe you're not over there
you're like so good
and you like work so hard

#11
yeah seriously

#13
sí sí señor es pollo loco

#8
(looking offstage)
they're laughing
they're all laughing

they all look

#2
(looking off)
what are they writing down

all look off

#8
oh my god
did he sign them?
what if he signed them?

#7
don't be a moron
he wouldn't sign them right now
Dan had like a whole waiting period

#13
he probably just got their phone numbers

#11
oh my god
she's going to vomit

#13
no

#8
omigosh

#7
she's going to hurl all over his clipboard

#2
hold it in! hold it in

#11
she's keeping it together

#13
it's staying down

#7
they're shaking hands again

#8
omigosh

#46 and #14 and #00 jog back on

#11
how was it?

#8
what'd they say?

#00 *runs off to vomit*

#13
thar she blows!

#11
c'mon c'mon
tell us the good stuff

#46
he was very nice

#14
he just wanted our phone numbers
and like emails

#13
cool
cool

#2
where's he from?

#46
um Texas A & M?
I think?

#7
(*she thinks*)

#14
yeah
Texas A & M

#11
(*furious*)
. . . that's so fun!

#46
. . . yeah!

#14
(to #46, directed at #7)
you should tell them what he told you

#8
what
omigosh what

#46
oh nothing

#14
(to #7)
she's being modest
he was like
"that bicycle kick coulda been on ESPN"

#46
haha
yeah

#7
. . . you've played soccer before
right?

#46
what do you mean?

#13
did you play O.D.P?

#46
O.D.P?

#11
Olympic Development Program

#8
like there's no way this is your first time on a team
there's like SO no way

#46
(laughing a little)
no
the Olympics?
definitely not
this is actually my first team
with like jerseys

#13
(suspicious)
really dude?

#46
yes

#11
but that's
you're so

#2
good

#46
oh I mean but I've played before
I've played a lot

#2
where?

#46
uh well
all over the world actually

#13
WHAAAAAAT??

#46
yeah
my mom travels a lot for her job so
we move uh
pretty much constantly

#14
whoa

#46
and everyone plays football
um soccer
like everywhere
like Jakarta Krakow La Paz uh Kampala
even if you don't speak the language
so it's uh
it's a good way to uh
make
(self-conscious) friends

#11
. . . wait what does your mom do?

#13
does she like work for the CIA?

#8
omigosh is your mom a spy??

#46
haha
no
no
she's um
she's a travel writer

#11
that's something you can actually be?

#46
I guess so
not a lot of people do it

#8
wait wait wait
is she like famous??

#46
(*shrugs*)
not unless you're really into travel writing

#11
so like where have you gone

#46
oh um all over
we just got back from Morocco
before that Cambodia

#13
you've been to Cambodia??

#46
yeah
I um I think I told you that

#2
whoa

#13
holy shit man
so like you know all about the (*mispronounces*) Khmer Rouge

#11
Khmer Rouge

#46
(*shrugs*)
sorta

Khmer Rouge

#7
wait if you've been to all these places
then like why the fuck are you living here?

#46
oh
my grandma lives here
she's really sick
she has emphysema?

#8
. . . oh my gosh

#00 reenters

#46
hey um
sorry about your leg

#7
it fucking sucks

#46
you shoulda been out there today

#7
I know

#46
you're a really good striker

#7
yeah
I know
. . .you looked good out there

#46
(excited)
really?

#7
(sorta aggressive)
yeah really

#46
(a little moved)
thanks

#8
I mean obviously duh you were so awesome

#46
(to #7)
that means a lot
that's
thanks

#2
oh!

#11
what?

#2
I forgot
hold on

#7
whatever don't be weird about it

#8
thank god you came back from Cambodia you know   *#2 jogs off*
that's all I gotta say
thank god

#46
(to #7, familiar)
man you've had a rough couple of months huh?

#7
what do you mean?

#46   #13
you know the uh   (coughs)
the um thing around Thanksgiving?

#7
what?

#25   #11
ladies let's uh   yeah!   #8
let's move on to passing   that sounds great

                                                  #25
#46   let's do it
it's just great that you have such a supportive boyfriend

#7
the fuck you know about my boyfriend?

(to #14)
wait
are you fucking serious?

#14
hey
no
that's not

#7
it was just PLAN B you dicks

#14
I didn't tell anyone I swear

#13
(that's what I said)

#7
you know what?
fuck you guys
fuck this
what I do with my body is my own fucking business
I don't need this
I quit

#11
(shut up)

#14
you're not going to fucking quit

#7
you're right
I'm not
I fucking love soccer
maybe I'll just join BLUE STORM

#14
fuck you

#7
fuck YOU I INVITED you
and you MOPED like a little PUSSY

#14
you LEFT ME ALONE with that guy

#7
he LIKED you
and you said he was HOT

#14
yeah but you just like
you ABANDONED me
to go FUCK your STUPID FUCKING BOYFRIEND
so / very LOUDLY!

#7
/I FUCKING LOVE HIM OK???
AND I NEVER GET TO SEE HIM!
/EVER!

#14
/and then you SKIIED on your fucking SPRAINED ANKLE

#7
I HOPE YOU FUCKING ROT YOU MISERABLE

#2 *runs back on holding a scarf*

#2
I made you a—

blackout

Time-Out

#00 lies facedown in the middle of the field

the gymnasium is silent

a long while

she bolts up

her eyes are red

she spills open the bag of balls
kicks each ball offstage in a fury

she is panting and wound up and crying

she tears her shirt off
and sinks to her knees

in a black sports bra
she holds her shirt
and screams

Week Six—We Are The Wolves

#46 sits in the middle of the field holding her phone
#11 stands at the edge wearing headphones

they stare at each other
*#46 sneezes**

#11

. . .

. . .

. . .

hey

#46
hey!

#11 looks around and takes out her headphones

#11
have you been here?
long?

#46
couple of minutes

#11

. . .

. . .

#46
really just got here

#11
uh huh

#46

. . .

---

*#46 has a cold this week

#11
. . .

#46
. . .

#11
. . .

#46
how have you been
since the uh

#11
good

#46
. . .

#11
. . .

#46
good

#11
. . .
well
uh
no
i don't know
I'm uh
probably not good

#46
yeah
yeah
. . .
probably not

#11
. . .

#46
. . .

#11
how about you

#46
oh
you know

#46
. . .

#11
. . .

#46
I got the cold that was going around

#11
that sucks

#46
yeah
it's ok

#11
want some Emergen-C?

#46
oh
no

#11
it helps

#46
I think it's a placebo

#11
. . .

#46
. . .

#11
. . .

#46
so you think we have to forfeit?

#11
oh
yeah
I mean
probably

#46
. . .

#11
. . .

#46
. . .

#46
I guess unless anyone else shows

#11
yeah

#46
we need six?

#11
six
yeah

#46
cool

#11
. . .

#46
four to go!

#11
. . .

#46
. . .

#11
. . .

#46
. . .
have you uh
have you seen everyone

#11
(*nods*)
at school and stuff

#46
that's good

#11
yeah
. . .
it's been weird

#46
yeah
. . .
. . .
is everyone uh
ok?

#11
I uh
I don't really

#8 enters
she has a big zit

#8
hi!

#46
hey!

#11
hey

#8
um is anyone else here?

#11
no

#8
are we still on?

#11
I don't know

#8
alright

#8 sighs and sits down
#11 is still standing

#8
so I guess now we're what
we're 5-2?

#46
2?

#8
Fusion and the forfeit

#11
yeah

#46
forfeit?

#11
um
last week?

#46
oh
. . .
that counts?

#11
I think so

pause

#8
boo

pause

#8
(texting)
people better get their asses out here

pause

#8
(looks up)
can I just say
this is like so weird

#46
yeah

#8
it's like
really really weird
. . .
i keep crying?
. . .
i can't stop uh
but I do that all the time
so uh

pause

#11
my dad keeps wanting to talk about it
like even in the car over here he was like
trying to talk about it
but I'm like
Not
Interested
I don't want to
I don't want to talk about it

#46
huh

pause

#11
I've talked about it

#8
yeah

#11
it's like
all I'm talking about

pause

#11
especially when it's like
I'm driving
and he's like
trying to pump the break in the passenger seat
it just feels like
I don't know
like
. . .
disrespectful

pause

#11
anyways

pause

#11
I'm just like
could you be my dad for a sec and not my therapist?
you know?

#8
(*checking her phone*)
that sucks

#46
wait I thought your mom was a therapist

#11
they're both therapists

#46
really?

#11
I don't wanna talk about it

pause

#8
you got your permit?

#11
oh
yeah

#8
lucky

#11
yeah
it's um
it's ok
it's ok

pause

#8
AHH!!

they both look at her, concerned

#8
this zit is SO HUGE!

pause

#8
it like hurts!
you know when they like hurt?

#46
yeah

pause

#8
I just want to like
blast it off my face

pause

#46
it's not so bad

pause

#8
it's huge

pause

#8
I like stayed home from school yesterday cause it was so huge
I woke up and I was like nope

#8 picks her face
sighs

#8
everyone else better show up

pause

#46
how's Alex doing?

#11 and #8 exchange a look

#11
she's uh
not great
you know

#46
yeah

#8
really not great

pause

#11
Kristen told me she hasn't gone back to school since

#8
yeah
I heard that too

#46
who's Kristen?

#8
(surprised)
omigosh you don't know Kristen?

#11
oh she's on the travel team

#46
there's more girls on the travel team?

#11
oh yeah

#8
loads more

#46
they don't play indoor?

#8
nah
they have like other stuff you know

#46
like what

#11
um Kristen plays basketball for St. Albert

#8
and Mariana plays basketball for East High

#11
Emma P. and Jessica do ski team

#8
which is so dumb
there are like so many injuries

#11
Taylor's recovering from surgery

#8
Ari's recovering from surgery

#11
Lily's recovering from surgery

#8
and Emma
uh
what's Emma doing?

#11
Emma P?

#8
no no Emma B.

#11
ohhh
Emma B. wanted to be in the "school play"

eye roll

#8
how could I forget

#11
she plays like an old German guy
a watchmaker or something
(*in accent*) haven't you heard her German accent

#8
isn't she like Jewish?

#11
I know
we sit together in calc
and she keeps like whispering
"don't you have ze guts to do vat you seenk ees right?"

#8
oh man

#11
she's so pumped
she like gets to wear a moustache

#8
oh yeah I saw that on Instagram

#11
the biggest Instawhore

#46
I think I met her at the service

pause

#8
I keep looking at that picture
with the orange slices

#11
I can't
it freaks me out too much

#8
I can't stop checking it

#2 *and* #00 *walk on*

#2   #00
hey!   hi!

#8
oh great you made it

#11
hey guys

#2
yeah her mom gave me a ride

#00
wow

#2
it's so good to see you guys

#00
we almost have a full roster

#11
yeah
wow

#00
one more and we can play
according to regulations

#46
that rocks

#00
(to #46)
haven't seen you for a while

#46
yeah

#2
how've you been?

#46
oh
it's been
yeah
sorta
sorta lonely
. . .
just sitting in my yurt uh
I uh
missed you guys
. . .
(to #00)
you're um
you're talking?

#00
huh?
oh
yeah
ha
I guess I am

#11
you feel ok?

#00
I don't really know
I haven't thought about it

#8
do you feel like you have to . . .?

#00
no
no
I guess I uh
interesting
I think I don't feel as stressed?

#2
about what

#00
about like
like people scoring on me
missing the ball
seeing it pass through my fingers
or like penalty kicks
or like corner kicks
or a shoot-out even
or just like losing
losing the game
it's not
I visualize a lot
I'm pretty much always visualizing
during warm-ups
at night when I can't sleep
when I noodle around on the sax
but
it doesn't seem so . . . scary
right now
I guess

#11
cool

#00
or maybe I think we're gonna forfeit
so it just hasn't hit me yet
. . .
um so how are you guys?

#11
ok

#8
ok

#46
yeah

pause

#2
this is so weird

#8
that's what I said
it's really weird being here

pause

#11
she shouldn't have worn headphones

#8
yeah but

#11
she shouldn't have
it's so dangerous
she knew that

#00
that guy should have scraped his windshield
or like defrosted it

#11
right I know but if she had heard him?

#2
guys

pause

#46
hey is that the Hornets?

they all look off

#11
again?

#2
I guess so

pause

#00
I would love to win right now
I would really really love to win

they stare at the Hornets

#46
anyone wanna pass?

#2
. . . sure

they get a ball and pass
silence for a little bit

#8
(*singing to* Schoolhouse Rock)
WE THE PEOPLE
IN ORDER TO FORM A MORE PERFECT UNION

#8/#00
ESTABLISH JUSTICE
ENSURE DOMESTIC TRANQUILITY

#8/#00/#2
PROVIDE FOR THE COMMON DEFENSE
PROMOTE THE GENERAL WELFARE AND
SECURE THE BLESSINGS OF LIBERTY

#8/#00/#2/#11
TO OURSELVES AND OUR POSTERITY
TO ORDAIN AND ESTABLISH
THIS CONSTITUTION
FOR THE
UNITED STATES OF
AMERICA

#8
that was fun!

                        #00
                        talk about a deep cut

#46
what was that

#11
um the preamble

#00
we had to memorize it

#2
in fifth grade

#11
and like perform it one by one in front of the whole school

#8
in assembly

#00
it was my nightmare

#2
it was my Nam

#8
people say that all the time but I don't get it

#2
it's something my grandpa says about my grandma's cooking

#8
like nom?
like nom nom nom?

#2
no I think like um

#00
Vietnam

#11
they're talking about Vietnam
like something's really hard it's like Vietnam

#25 *walks on*
she has a buzzcut

#25
hey!

#8
OMIGOSH

#11
whoa!

#00
oh my god

#2
wow!

#46
oooh

#25
sorry I didn't think we were playing

#11
holy shit!

#00
you look so great

#25
what

#2
your hair

#25
oh
yeah
how long have you guys been here?

#46
don't worry about it

#8
what did you do to your hair??

#25
oh I
buzzed it
sorry
I thought we were going to have to forfeit so I

#46
I think we're good
right
we have six

#25
yeah
wow
I guess so
. . . Coach here?

#11
haven't seen him

#25
oh right
it's his weekend on base

#8
wow he gave us that schedule so long ago

#25
ok
. . .
ok
I'll go talk to the ref . . .
I guess we're playing
I guess we're on

#25 jogs off

#11
man I can't believe we're actually gonna play

#2
yeah
I can't tell if I want to or not

#8 gets a text

#00
I'm so ready you guys
I've like never felt this ready

#8
NO!!!

#8 bursts into tears
they all stare at her

#2
(going to comfort her)
hey
shhh

#8
(through sobs)
Tulsa

#2
it's ok
it's ok

#8
(through sobs)
Tulsa
it's in Tulsa

#2
shh

#11
what's in Tulsa?

#8
nationals
they're in Tulsa

#46
what?

#00
that blows

#11
what happened to Miami?

#8
(nodding)
Emma just texted me

#2
. . . that really really stinks
but you know what?
someday you'll get to go to Miami

#13 jogs in

#13
helloooo good people

#11
look who made it

#13
of course I did
of course of course
I thought we would forfeit but nopedy nope nope

#2
now we have seven

#46
an alternate!

#13
(re: #8)
is she ok?

#2
nationals are in Tulsa

#8
(sniffling)
I'm never going to go to Disneyworld

#2
don't say that

#13
yeah
yeah
hahahahaha
yeah

#11
. . . are you on crack or something?

#13
um
yeah
no
totally
haha
no
I'm great
I uh
haven't been sleeping
very much but uh
coupla asthma attacks
but
yeah I'm good
all good

#25 *runs back on*

#25
ok guys
it's cool
we're on

#13
dude!!
your hair!!

#25
oh
yeah

#13
dude!

#2
why'd you do it??

#25
oh I uh guess I wanted a change
it's so easy in the morning

#11
I bet

#13
whoa

#8
did like a barber do it?

#25
no
I actually
I did it myself

#25   #13
(to #8)   whoa whoa whoa
are you ok?

#8
nationals are in Tulsa

#25
really?

#13
wait you gave yourself a buzzcut??   #2
                                        wow

#8
like Mulan

#25
(nods)
haha yeah
with my dad's razor

#13
Coach Frank's razor rides again!

#11
you did that all by yourself?

#25
yeah
yeah
well I guess
I guess like Louise helped

#13
. . . Louise?

#25
yeah
she uh
she's shaved her head before so I thought she'd
and she like got the back of my neck
my uh she called them my
(blushing) my blind-spots

#2
. . . can I feel it?

#25
uh
sure

#2 feels it

#2
it's soft
it's so soft

#13
let me see

#8 feels

#8
omigosh it's like a baby duck it's so soft

#11 feels

#11
that feels so cool

#13 feels

#13
wow
totally like a baby duck

#00 feels

#00
you look really awesome

#25
thanks
it's so easy I just like shower and that's it
no ponytail
no hair icicles

#2
maybe I'll shave my head

#25
yeah!
yeah
. . . well you guys wanna warm-up?

#11
yeah

#13
yeah

#8
yeah

they get in a circle and begin their warm-up
total silence for a while
it feels really good to do the warm-up again

#11
(looking at audience)
guys is that Coach Patrick?

#8
omigosh
it's Coach Patrick

#13
whoa there are a lotta people over there all of a sudden

#25
oh
yeah
my dad like texted all the other parents
on their little group text

#2
I thought he gave a really beautiful speech

#11
Coach Patrick?
yeah

#8 waves

#8
guys
guys he's waving

they all wave and shout hi/hello/etc

#13
oh wowww who's that weirdo witch lady sitting next to him

#46
that's um
that's my mom

#13
oh
. . . right on right on

#00
cool cape

#46
yeah
she's never come to a game before
I'm sorta nervous

#46 waves at her

#2
hey isn't that Louise?

#25
(blushing)
yeah!
she came for like
moral support

#11
cool

#25
yeah
. . . she like
she's lost like a lot of
like her older brother
she um found him in their garage
so uh
she's been pretty cool
actually
she's been pretty cool

pause

#13
I've never like
I've never had anyone

#11
like not even a grandparent?

#13
no
well I guess
like some beta fish but
I mean I know people but I've never gone to a funeral, you know?
or hadn't
I guess

#00
my grandma died a few years ago
my dad's mom

#25
I don't have any grandparents

#11
me neither

#46
I just have my one grandma
but I don't know my dad so
maybe I have two

pause

#2
my neighbor died a few years ago
he was really nice
he used to let me and my brothers and sisters come over and feed the birds

some of them look at #8 expectantly

#8
(chipper)
hey! there's Kevin!

#13
(thrilled)
dude! what a doofus!

#11
hey Ari and Lily are here too

#8
yeah
I texted like everyone I know

#2
cool

pause

\#25
she shouldn't have worn headphones

\#00
he should have like
he should have defrosted you know

\#2
guys

\#13
she shouldn't have gone for a run at 6 a.m.
with snow on the ground
what sorta what sorta NUTjob does that

#7 hobbles on the field

\#7
sup bitches

slight pause

\#8
hey Alex

\#2
hi

\#11
hey

\#00
hey girl

\#7
(to #25)
your hair!

#25 smiles and nods

\#13
how you doing?

#7
you know
ok

pause

#7
fucking weird to be here

#8
yeah

#13
yeah

pause

#7
(*trying hard*)
you guys have a huge fucking crowd!

#11
yeah

#8
haha

#7
it's huge!

#25
did you see Coach Patrick?

#7
yeah
yeah

pause

#7
keep stretching!
I just wanted to you know
say hey

awkward silence

#46
are you ok?

#7
yeah
I'm uh
yeah
you know

pause

#7
(brightly)
Dan's here

#2
yeah?

#7
uh huh
he took some time off school

#25
where is he?

#7
he's parking

#2
that's great
that's so great

#7
yeah

awkward pause

#25
so uh
did you hear
nationals are in Tulsa?

#7
really?
(laughing)
 that blows

they all laugh with her

#7
guess it's good there's no chance in hell I'll make it this year

#13
haha yeah

SOCCER MOM *walks on the field*
she is manic with grief

SOCCER MOM
hi!
hi gals!

a small collective hi

wow
you look so
wow!
my god!
it's you guys!
it's our gals!
you're not getting any younger
you know?
you all look so
and it's just
it is so good to see you
just
like
like
like so good

a pause
she lets out a sharp laugh

I said
ha
listen to me

ha
"like"
ha
"like" "like" "like"
in our house we have a quarter jar
Alex I know you've seen it
a quarter for every "like"
and for "um" every "um"
and the oh the what do you
the going up? at the end? of the sentence?
what is that
but
they hate it
the girls
they just hate it
and I've tried to explain
if you're saying something is "like" something
then it isn't the same
it's just "like" it
and if you say that
and you hem and you haw and you um and you make everything?
a question?
then no matter how you know awesome
how brilliant your thought is
no one will ever take you seriously
because you sound like an idiot
and one time I said
I was mad
I was really
she didn't do the dishes or was texting at dinner or uh
(trying to remember) I don't uh
I don't
funny

she is lost in thought
then sudden and snapping

"MEGAN you say "LIKE" because you don't know ANYTHING about ANYTHING"
I said
"ANYTHING about ANY"
I was
I was really
and uh

SOCCER MOM
Megan said to me
"like you do??"
"like YOU DO??"
and I
do I?
do I know anything about?

she smiles and looks at the girls from very far away
sudden, to #2

honey
are you eating?
are you eating honey?
you've gotten so skinny
I didn't even recognize
just as long as you're eating ok?
ok
. . . ok

she gets a little self-conscious

now we want to see a win out there!
today!
win! win! win!
lots of fans
Big Fans
longtime fans came out just to see you!
how cool is that?
right?
so cool
Frank texted me and I was like
"I am In"
so none of that
none of that stuff with the Fusion
let's see some uh some smart soccer today
smart passing smart listening smart eyes
I've seen so many games
you have no idea
so many Saturdays and tournaments and practices and

And Megan's watching
Megan is

sudden and distraught

oh
oh no I
I for
oh shoot I
I forgot to
shoot
from the trunk
the trunk!
oh god
I'm sorry
I'm so sorry
I'm
I'm so so
it's not
ok ok I'll be back in a jiff
I just forgot to
ok
I'm sorry
ok
it's ok
it's ok

SOCCER MOM *hurries off*

a long, long silence

whistle

#25
(very small)
ok
let's uh
. . .
uh
me and #2 on defense to start
you're goalie
#46 striker
and uh
#11 and #13 on mid

whistle

#7
good luck guys

#7 starts to leave

#25
wanna do the cheer?

#7 hobbles over as they huddle up
silence
it starts as a whisper
and grows louder and louder
until it feels rabid and raw and Bacchic

#11/#25/#13/#46/#2/#7/#8/#00
we
are
the wolves
we are the wolves

we
are
the wolves
we are the wolves

we
are
the wolves
we are the wolves

we
are
the WOLVES
we are THE WOLVES

WE
ARE
THE WOLVES
WE ARE THE WOLVES

WE
ARE
THE WOLVES
WE ARE THE WOLVES

WE
ARE
THE WOLVES
WE ARE THE WOLVES

WE
ARE
THE WOLVES
WE ARE THE WOLVES

WE
ARE
THE WOLVES
WE ARE THE WOLVES

SOCCER MOM *walks on*
she holds a Ziploc of orange slices

they howl

they stop

they pant

they see her

or they don't

END OF PLAY